SO-ELL-813

Much larger in content than it may
at first appear, this little book contains
the power to transform your life
by transforming your thoughts.

Seeds of Consciousness

Affirmations For Daily Living

by Louise-Diana

Design & illustrations
by Nancy Steinman

DeVorss Publications

Seeds of Consciousness: Affirmations for Daily Living
Copyright ©1999
By Louise-Diana

All rights reserved. No part of this book may be reproduced or transmitted
in any form without permission in writing from the publisher,
except by a reviewer who may quote brief passages for review purposes.

ISBN: 0-87516-724-1
Library of Congress Catalog Number: 98-74807

First Edition, 1999

Devorss & Company, *Publisher*
P.O. Box 550
Marina del Rey, CA 90294

Printed in the United States of America

About the Author

The creator of the personal growth concept <u>Inner Fitness</u>, **Louise-Diana** is a respected authority in the field of personal effectiveness. She helps people to take charge of their lives by achieving balance and inner harmony.

She is a yoga therapist, a certified clinical hypnotherapist, a motivational speaker and is licensed as a Science of Mind practitioner. She is currently enrolled in the Holmes Institute to become an ordained Minister.

In <u>Seeds of Consciousness: Affirmations for Daily Living</u> her powerful suggestions will help you use the power of positive thought to transform your life.

Learn how to overcome obstacles to success and increase your overall happiness and satisfaction with life through self-confirmation. You will be amazed at the results.

Acknowledgments

I dedicate this book to my mother and father, who always made me feel special. They recognized the light within me and, even though it might have blinded them at times, they made sure it always burned bright.

With affection, I thank my closest friends, Saralyn Myers and Darren Star, who have moved with me over the threshold of youthful impatience into the deep, quiet waters of intimate friendship and a life of grace and more substance.

I thank the power and presence of Spirit for showing me my life's purpose.

Table of Contents

Self-Empowerment 1

Creativity 15

Spirituality 19

Success 25

Business & Career 33

Prosperity 37

Health 41

Relationships 59

Higher Learning 67

Sports 73

Index 80

We live in a wonderful era – a time of great discovery and progress. Yet many people believe that times are hard and that there are few opportunities to succeed. Nothing could be further from the truth.

Success is not a set of circumstances as much as it is a set of attitudes. Even in times of great difficulty, there are always people who overcome adversity and become successful. Success does not come easily, though. It takes a great deal of energy and enthusiasm. Both attributes are essential to reach goals and overcome minor setbacks.

The first step, though, is to be grateful for what you already have. We often overlook accomplishments, such as a solid job or good health, because we are obsessed with trying to achieve what we don't yet possess. Think about what you already have before you start each day.

Be enthusiastic about everything you do. Enthusiasm is that state of exuberance in which all things seem possible. It is what drives each of us to pursue our dreams.

Learn continually. You possess an inner wisdom that enables you to determine who your teachers are and what they have to teach you. To find teachers who will help you to become successful, carefully study the behavior and actions of those you admire a great deal. Look for someone with honesty, integrity and compassion, since these are the basic ingredients of a truly successful person.

Finally, stick with it. Perseverance is the difference between success and defeat. Reaching a goal may require repeated attempts. Each attempt brings you closer to achieving the objective. Listen to the voice within, urging you to "...try, try again." Remain constant to your purpose, idea or task in the face of obstacles and discouragement.

Use this book for motivation, reinforcement and enlightenment. Use it with the knowledge that we are all on a journey to find our Higher Selves. Namasté.

How to use this book

Close your eyes and take a long, deep breath.

Relax, grow very still and
listen to your heartbeat within.

Choose the affirmation that fits your needs.
Read it first silently and then aloud.

Remember in quietness and
confidence shall be your strength.

Your attitude will make this day what it becomes.

Self-Empowerment

Enthusiasm & Motivation

I feel great excitement about life.
I am a doer and a self-starter. I exude boundless energy.
I appreciate my life.

Stop Procrastinating

I do what I need to do now. I meet deadlines.
Every day I achieve more and more. I make things happen.
I love the reward of accomplishment.
I act decisively. I am a doer.

Decide Now! Decide Right!

I make my own choices. I am decisive.
My mind quickly and clearly evaluates options.
I always decide what is best for me.

Becoming Assertive

I have the power and commitment to assert myself.
I am positively confident.
I speak up. I value my opinions.

Rescripting the Child Within

I accept and forgive myself. I release guilt.
I regularly get a new lease on life. I know life is a school.
I accept what I learn. I am whole.

Neat & Clean

I feel the satisfaction of creating order around me.
I am neat and organized. I love cleanliness and order.
I put things in their place. I have a clear mind.

Have it All

I develop a deeply positive expectation of good,
and I draw it to me. I enjoy life.
I am energetic. I am enthusiastic.
I am intuitive. I am prosperous. I am lucky.

Freedom from Fears

I overcome my fears and experience life to its fullest.
I am free of fear. I am optimistic.
I am powerful. I am okay. Fear is gone.

Dissolving Anger

I release all anger and enjoy peace within. I forgive myself.
I forgive others. I find humor in life.
My emotions are positive. I am calm. I am in harmony.

Accepting Change

I learn to accept, appreciate and make the best of change.
Change is opportunity. Change is exciting.
All things change. I live in harmony.

Forgiving and Letting Go

I free myself from yesterday and experience joy today.
I am accepting. I am forgiving. I am joyous.
All occurs with purpose. I live in peace.

Surviving Abuse

I am free of guilt. I am free of shame.
I am free of blame. I am good. I release anger.
I am loved and accepted.

Effective Communication

I express myself with confidence, ease and clarity.
I speak well. My thoughts flow freely.
I am self-assured. I am an effective speaker.

Ultra-Positive Self-Image

I feel great about myself, my abilities and my life.
I am brilliant and capable. I am unlimited.
I exude confidence. I am a leader.

Confidence

I create a dynamic state of self-confident expectancy.
I feel good about myself. I am sincere and confident.
I do everything with confidence. I am liked by other people.

Radiating Warmth & Charisma

I glow with loving warmth and charisma.
My charismatic personality draws people to me.
People enjoy my company.

Great Sense of Humor

I inject joy and humor into my life each day.
I enjoy laughing. My sense of humor is keen.
I love to smile and make others smile.
I am light-hearted. Life is exciting. Life is fun.

High Self-Esteem

I enhance confidence, eliminate self-sabotage and
create success. I believe in myself.
I release all thoughts and relationships that
no longer serve my highest good. I trust myself.
I am focused and attuned to my goals. I am a winner.

Becoming Motivated

I stimulate my mind and body with energy and
momentum for action. I act on my positive thoughts.
I feel the power of purpose and motivation. I take action.
I am empowered by the energy of my creative thoughts.

Impulse Control

I control my emotions. I think things through.
I cancel the negative. I respect myself.
I am honest. I am in control.

Enduring Patience

I deepen my compassion, understanding and patience.
I am compassionate with myself and with others.
I release impatience and judgment.
I am at peace. I feel the strength of patience.

Trust

I let confidence and love replace fear and doubt.
I calm my mind, my body and my spirit by
experiencing the calmness of trust.
I am comfortable with the new and the unknown.
I live in a state of trust and wholeness of being.

Recharge

I recharge my mind, body and spirit with
vitality and clarity of purpose.
I energize myself for increased mental awareness.
I refresh my mind with new ideas and creative thought.
At the end of the day, I feel rested and renewed.

Release

I release self-defeating behaviors that prevent
balance and good health. I release and let go of
addictions to people and things that keep me
from my highest purpose. I experience new, positive
patterns that nurture my mind, body and spirit.
I choose to be free and vibrantly alive.

Winning Self-Image and Self-Confidence

I believe life is good to me. I feel good about myself.
My personal power makes me confident.
I am absolutely worthy.

Willpower

I am firm in my decisions.
I feel strongly committed. I am highly confident.
My strong willpower brings me pleasure.

Creativity

Memory Power

I stimulate my powers of recall and retention.
I recall and retain all the information I need.
My memory serves me well. I use my memory effortlessly.

Unleash Creativity

My mind generates many ideas. I have great creative energy.
My ideas manifest themselves in reality.
My creativity contributes to the lives of others.
I act on my creative ideas. I am truly creative.

Dreamwork

I tap into the hidden power of my dreams.
I easily recall the important messages from my dreams.
I solve problems through my dreams.
I use my dreams as a tool for learning.

Increase Creativity

Creative ideas flow to me and from me freely and easily.
I am creative and ingenious.
All aspects of my present and my future are
filled with creative thoughts, words and actions.

Imagination & Visualization

I stimulate my powerful imagination and open new pathways
for thoughts and actions. I see mental images.
I see solutions. I notice details and hold vivid images.
I channel inspiration into action.

Intuition

I am an intuitive, creative human being.
I access my powerful right brain for problem-solving.
I allow my intuition to guide me with information and insight.
My intuition serves, balances and harmonizes my life.

Spirituality

Enlightenment

I allow my highest good to unfold in my spiritual journey.
I am an open channel for light and love.
I experience enlightenment at the highest levels.
My blessings are unlimited.

Meditation

A meditative state comes easily and effortlessly to me.
I still my mind, calm my body and renew my spirit.
I am receptive to the highest thoughts and teachings.
I meditate with calmness and clarity.

Miracles

I tap the power of miracles by accepting the
truly miraculous nature of life. I am eternal.
I am a miracle. God's presence resides within me.

Awakening

I develop my psychic powers and extrasensory awareness.
I open up. I trust my impressions. My feelings expand.
My senses are powerful. I vibrate energy.
I am wise. I am psychic.

Open Up To a Higher Power

I am in touch with the higher power within me.
I am a creation of the Divine. I was created perfectly.
I am humbly grateful. I trust in a higher power.

Metaphysical Oneness

I experience the oneness of the
Kingdom of Heaven within me. I live in the Divine.
I live in oneness. I live in balance. I can do anything.
My mind is one with the Universal Mind.

Centering

I enjoy a beautiful center of serenity and harmony.
I am master of myself. I experience good in all.
I learn without resistance. Only beauty surrounds me.
I accept. I allow. I live in joy.

Love, Light & Life

I feel the radiant presence of love wherever I am.
Eternal love and light are my blessings.
I radiate peace, balance and harmony.
God's will is my perfect will. I am a child of God.

Consciousness Expansion

I open the unconscious regions of my mind to
collective thought. I was created in God's image.
I am a being of the light. All that I do is in love.
I expand and open my mind.

Higher Self

I nurture my inner self for balance, purpose and vision.
I allow the wisdom and love of my Higher Self
to nurture and guide me to my heart's desire.
I am one with my Higher Self.

Success

Efficient & Organized

I set priorities. I am naturally efficient. I work smart.
I appreciate my ability to organize. I am thorough.
I gain more free time by getting my life organized.
My life flows with harmony.

Setting & Achieving Goals

I accept myself as a person who gets things done.
I reach all my goals. My thoughts are clear.
I focus on specific goals and guarantee their realization.
I stay on course. I achieve the best.

Winning Personality

I like people, and they like me.
It is natural for me to be a winner.
I strongly believe in myself. People respect my opinions.
I have a magnetic personality that attracts others.

Personal Success

I eliminate self-sabotage and surpass my goals.
I confidently achieve all my goals and heart's desires.
Success comes to me easily. I release any beliefs or
obstacles standing in the way of my success.
I experience success daily in new, creative ways.

Focus & Concentration

I use full mental power to target peak performance.
I am centered and productive.
I sharpen my single-minded attention for rapid results.
I focus my mind and my energy with ease and clarity.
I accomplish what I focus on. I see clearly.

Managing Your Time

I enjoy organizing my time. I am punctual.
I quickly eliminate time-wasters. I get more done in less time.
My entire life is balanced and organized.

Effective Speaking

I am a compelling speaker. I speak with enthusiasm.
My ideas are worth communicating.
I enjoy gesturing – it is natural and appropriate.
My thoughts are clear and well expressed.

Powerful Recall

I have perfect memory and recall.
I build short- and long-term memory.
I recall all the information I need, whenever I need it.
I release stored knowledge and information.
My brain is a wondrous storehouse of information
which I use effortlessly.

Winning State of Mind

I have the power to win. Winning comes naturally to me.
I have great inner courage. I am alert and perceptive.
I appreciate all my successes.

Positive Mental Attitude

I guarantee positive results by implanting positive beliefs.
I think positively. I expect only the positive.
I can do anything. I am a winner.

Strong Commitment

I strengthen my ability to keep promises.
I experience integrity through my commitments.
I decide with clarity and commitment.
I release doubt. I choose wisely.
I am strengthened by my decisions.

Unlimited Personal Power

I unleash incredible feelings of self-confidence and mastery.
I tap into my higher power. I imagine success in detail.
I am powerful. I am a leader. I make it happen.

Igniting Enthusiasm & Motivation

I feel invigorated, motivated and alive.
I act enthusiastically. I follow through.
I am enthused about my goals. I feel great.

Learning

I learn quickly and effortlessly. I build a foundation of
confidence and wisdom through knowledge.
Every experience is an opportunity for success and learning.
I choose to learn. I use my learning wisely.

Business & Career

Successful Sales

I generate sales. My income rises higher and higher.
My timing is perfect. I instinctively say the right thing.
I overcome objections with ease. I am a strong closer.
I am persuasive and successful. I believe in myself and
my products. My sales benefit me and other people.

Peak Performance

I achieve stress-free levels of high performance.
I am productive. I love my work.
I see the purpose of each task clearly.
I perform challenging tasks with energy and focus.
I know I am competent. I can handle all that I receive.

Freedom from Burnout

I enjoy my profession. I enjoy challenges.
I do what I can do. I remain balanced.
I treat myself well. I am detached from pressure.

Networking for Successful Sales

I am a super-successful networker. I enjoy selling.
I enjoy people. My confidence is unshakable.
I generate leads. I get referrals. I create success.

Strategic Planning

I gain clarity, mental focus and discipline each day.
I use strategic thinking to maximize my brain power.
I am a clear thinker. I am decisive. I see the whole picture.
I listen for the sound of possibilities.
I choose the best pathway for the best outcome.

Management Skills

I am skilled at managing people and tasks.
I am confident in my abilities.
My co-workers respect my decisions.
I am a good arbitrator. I act calmly and wisely.
My working environment flows smoothly.

Prosperity

Prosperity

I internalize positive beliefs of prosperity and abundance
at the deepest levels to turn my dreams into realities.
My prosperity manifests itself in many forms.
There is an infinite supply.

Abundance

My life is full of lavish, unfailing abundance.
Abundance flows to me from unexpected sources.
I create good with my riches.

Enjoying Success

I am a winner. I deserve prosperity and success.
I am rich in thought, word and deed.
I am blessed beyond my wildest dreams.

Successful Money Management

I take charge of my financial life with confidence.
I make wise decisions. I am thrifty. I am in control.
I plan. I learn. I save regularly. I spend wisely.
I expect prosperity.

High Potential

I use inner strength to create powerful feelings of self-worth.
I experience balance and harmony of mind,
body and emotions. I release stress. I release fear.
I use the unlimited potential of my mind to expand
my opportunities. I release any obstacle to my highest good.

Attracting Prosperity & Success

I attract limitless prosperity in every area of my life.
Prosperity comes to me easily. I create the income I desire.
I have the power to attract money. I am very successful.

Health

Appetite & Weight Control

I can control my appetite. Small portions satisfy me.
My metabolism maintains my ideal weight.
I am in charge of my life. I feel great.

Winning at Weight Loss

I can attain my ideal weight. I eat only when I am hungry.
I create healthful new eating and exercise habits.
I effortlessly shed unwanted weight. I am in good health.
My perfect weight and beautiful body are unfolding daily.

Stop Eating Junk Food

I refuse junk food. I enjoy nutritious foods.
I love eating fresh fruits and vegetables.
I eat only healthy snacks. I eat sensibly.

Reduce Cholesterol Naturally

My body is healthy. My cholesterol lowers to normal levels.
Cholesterol-reducing food brings me pleasure.
I refuse fatty foods. My body naturally balances.
I have inner peace.

Look Young! Feel Young!

My body continually regenerates and renews itself.
My mental abilities sharpen with the years.
I am flexible, adaptable and full of joy.
I am vibrant and defy the passage of time. I look young.
My body is strong. I feel youthful and happy.

Longevity, Vitality & Health

I create health in my body. All my organs function healthily.
My body has a strong immune system.
I continually renew in youth and health.
I am energized by living.

Joy of Pregnancy & Childbirth

Childbirth is a natural, beautiful experience.
I am filled with confidence during pregnancy and delivery.
My baby is a being of love.

Ultimate Relaxation and Freedom from Stress

I am balanced and at peace in body, mind and spirit.
Peace surrounds me. I create tranquility.
Comforting energy flows through me.
I relax my body and mind during periods of high intensity.
I handle all that I do with ease and comfort.
I release stress. I am at peace.

Radiant Good Health

I fill my entire being with life-enhancing energies and
facilitate physical well-being. I imagine and enjoy
good health daily. All of my organs, tissues and cells
work for me in perfect order and harmony.

Vitality & Energy

I enjoy peak performance and high energy mentally,
physically and emotionally. I am vibrantly alive.
I have more than enough energy to do everything.
I am an unlimited fountain of energy and vitality.
I am powerful. Energy surges through me.

Free from Depression

I am refreshed and uplifted by a fountain of good feelings.
I love living. I find humor all around me. I am blessed.
I choose happiness. Life is wonderful. I feel positive.

Imagine Health

I experience health and wholeness by visualizing
a sound mind and body. I imagine good health daily.
My body is blessed with perfect wholeness and health.
I enjoy unlimited good health.

Natural Pain Relief

I interrupt the pain cycle and receive extended relief.
I am relaxed. I am free of pain. Pain is gone.
My body feels comfortable. I feel good.

Powerful Immune System

I mobilize my body's own natural defenses to fight off disease.
My body creates helpful antibodies. I am healthy.
My immune system maintains health. I release diseases.
I accept perfect health. My body is perfect.

Relief from Arthritis

I am free of arthritis. Movement is easy.
I find relief through the power of my mind.
I eat the proper foods. My body regenerates itself.
My joints are loose. I am free of pain.

Freedom from Substance Abuse

I am drug-free. I fill my body only with healthy things.
I am strong and in control. I make wise choices.
I protect my health. I feel great. I am free.

Lower Blood Pressure

I displace my tension and agitation with quiet inward calm.
My body is perfect. My blood pressure is normal.
I am worry-free. I choose peaceful thoughts.
My cardiovascular system is healthy.

Forever Free of Cigarettes

I am free of smoking. Cigarettes are out of my life.
Cigarettes are distasteful and smell awful.
I am ready for clean lungs. I am in control.
I take care of my body. I live a smoke-free life.

Natural Self-Healing

I gain and maintain vibrant health through the
powerful healing forces of my mind.
My cells remember and produce health.
I am focused on health. I enjoy optimal health.

Headache Relief

I experience a soothing of the tension and
anxiety that cause my headaches.
I relax my scalp. I relax my throat. I breathe deeply.
I choose comfort. I feel great.

Relaxation

I am refreshed and renewed. I am worry-free.
I experience total relaxation. I am calm.
I am at peace with myself. I am at peace with the world.

Sleep Soundly

I fall asleep easily and enjoy deep, restful sleep all
night long. Sleep is effortless. Sleep restores my energy.
As I lie down to sleep I feel safe, secure and calm.
My dreams are pleasant and joyful. I sleep soundly.
I need less sleep and gain more time each day.

Freedom from Allergies

I am free from allergies. I breathe easily.
I find incredibly quick relief from any allergy.
I am healthy. I am relaxed. My body is perfect.

Clear Skin

My skin is young, clear and healthy.
My skin is elastic. My skin is vibrant and radiant.
I care for my skin. I eat properly. I am healthy.

Excellent Posture

I carry myself with confidence and project
a strong self-image. I stand erect. I sit erect.
I move with my head up and my shoulders back.
I am proud of my body.

Enjoying Exercise

Exercise is fun. I choose health. I care for myself.
I feel wonderful when I exercise regularly.
I am committed to my exercise program.
As I exercise, my endurance increases.
Exercise makes me feel confident and strong.

Freedom from Sugar

My craving for sweets is diminished. I eat properly.
I like vegetables. I like fruit. I avoid all processed sugar.
Food tastes great naturally. My health is improving.

Keen Vision

I improve my eyesight through my empowered mind.
I have good vision. I exercise my eyes. I care for my eyes.
My eyes are healthy. My eyes focus. Images are clear.

Freedom from Alcohol

I have the power to be free of alcohol.
I feel no craving for alcohol.
My obsession is gone. I naturally refuse alcohol.
Alcohol has no control over my life.

Accelerating Healing

Healing energy flows through me.
I am strong and healthy. My body quickly regenerates.
I feel healthier, stronger and better every day.
I have peace of mind.

Drug Prevention

I can make my own decisions.
I do not need drugs. I believe in myself. I trust myself.
I absolutely refuse drugs. Drugs have no hold over me.

Pain Reduction

My nerves and muscles automatically relax and release.
When I breathe deeply I automatically relax all over.
My mind knows how to turn off pain.
I appreciate my body.

Speeding Recovery after Injury or Operation

My body heals quickly and completely.
Every cell of my body renews.
My mind releases chemicals that help heal me.
I appreciate my body's healing. I am healthy and whole.

Body Beautiful

My mind power rejuvenates me.
I appreciate my body. My body is beautifully proportioned.
I radiate health and beauty. I have a healthy glow.
My body remolds into perfection.

Relationships

Sexual Responsiveness for Women
(Overcoming Frigidity)

I feel good about myself. I expect the best.
Touching and caressing arouse me sexually.
Sexual intimacy is a good and enjoyable experience for me.
I forgive and release all. I can let go.

Sexual Responsiveness for Men
(Overcoming Impotency)

I can perform well sexually.
I am sexually capable and naturally responsive.
I feel good about myself. I am secure and safe.
Every day I become more sexually confident.

Sexual Self-Confidence and Enjoying Intimacy

I am safe and secure in intimate relationships.
I express my feelings and affection openly with my lover.
I am able to give and receive sexually.
I accept my sexual self as a positive part of who I am.
I like to touch. I like to be touched. My body is beautiful.

Fulfillment in Love

I achieve intimacy and pleasure with my loving partner.
I experience fully the joy of connection and love.
My heart, my mind and my body are one with my beloved.
I expect the best. I experience ecstasy.

Connection

I create and renew loving relationships.
I connect with others through compassion, understanding
and loving communication. I experience the essence of love
and unity with all things at the deepest levels of my being.

Charisma

I develop the characteristics that naturally attract
others to me. I am humorous. I love people. I love life.
I am charming. People are my friends.

Positive Parenting

I am a great parent and nurture happy children.
I am patient. I am loving. I listen to my children.
I have fun with my children. I act wisely.
I teach my children by positive example.

Attracting The Right Love Relationships

I radiate the qualities I want in another person.
I attract my soulmate for a loving, fulfilling relationship.
I radiate warmth and friendship. I deserve the best.
The right relationships come to me.
I accept love into my life now.

Overcoming Shyness

I emerge from behind my fear of people
and enjoy an active social life.
I am unafraid of social situations. I like to talk.
I am completely at ease around all people.

Confidence with the Opposite Sex

I feel at ease around the opposite sex and end
self-sabotaging loneliness. I express my feelings easily.
Conversation is easy and natural for me.
People of the opposite sex like me and find me attractive.

Positive Relationships

I open my channels to understanding and
acceptance in all of my relationships.
I am loving. I listen intently.
It is easy to have good relationships.

Forgiveness

I forgive myself and others any regrets,
mistakes, hurts or anger. Others forgive me.
I am renewed and transformed by forgiveness.
I release and let go of any beliefs that keep me from
fully loving and forgiving myself and others.

Releasing Co-Dependent Patterns

I am independent. I respect myself.
I am worthy. I am responsible for myself.
I accept myself. I accept others.

Ending Self-Sabotage

I free myself of self-destructive beliefs and behaviors.
My life is unfolding according to a perfect plan.
I release all thoughts and relationships that
no longer serve my highest good.
I accept the gifts of life, love and joy.

Higher Learning

Powerful Memory

I have a powerful memory. My mind is quick and alert.
My memory serves me well. I retain all the information I need.
I increase my short- and long-term memory power.
Memory flows effortlessly.

Powerful Concentration

My concentration is uninterrupted.
I powerfully focus my mind. I concentrate easily.
My mental processes are sharp. I am focused and alert.
I boost my powers of concentration for greater success.

Getting Good Grades

My mind is quick and alert. I am naturally intelligent.
I have excellent reasoning ability. I express what I know easily.

Peak Learning

I learn easily. I remember what I read, hear and see.
I have a special ability to determine the most
important material to study. Learning is fun.

Accelerated Learning & Study

I fuel the powers of my mind to learn with speed and ease.
I focus. I read with comprehension. I listen intently.
I learn effortlessly.

Recall

I strengthen short- and long-term retention of information.
I recall the information I need whenever I need it.
My brain holds all the information I need.
I have perfect memory and recall.

Focus

I am clear in thinking, studying and communicating.
I am stress-free and focused on achieving my life-goals.
I am aware, productive and accomplish what I focus on.
I am centered. I see clearly.

Excel in Exams

I remove mental blocks, relieve anxiety and recall information easily. I am smart. I excel at tests. I remember easily. I am relaxed during tests. Answers come to me clearly.

Word Power

I gain greater mastery of language. I use words correctly. I have a powerful vocabulary. I speak well. I write well.

Becoming a Great Reader

I read with speed, ease and retention. Reading is easy. I read faster and faster. I concentrate when reading. I comprehend what I read. I am an accomplished reader.

Super Intelligence and Awakening Inner Genius

I develop my full potential by claiming the unlimited
resources of my inner mind. My mind is keen.
I am alert. I am intuitive. I dream solutions.
I am quick. I am insightful. I am a genius.

Hemispheric Brainpower (Using Both Halves of the Brain)

I balance both halves of my brain to heighten all my
mental activity and ability. I imagine with all my senses.
Everything around me becomes stimuli for growth.
I solve problems easily.

Sports

Winning Athletic Performance

I believe in myself. My moves are fast and accurate.
I have the power to win. My mind focuses powerfully.
My performance is flawless and automatic.

Yoga

My body is strong, flexible and fluid.
I breath easily into the flow of a pose.
I move beyond physical and mental blocks.
I use body, mind and spirit for perfect alignment.

Basketball

I perform under pressure. I am relaxed and in control.
I am a team player. I make every shot. I am a winner.

Baseball

I step into my swing. I am a great hitter.
My throw is fast and strong. I catch every ball.
I train my eyes to see every pitch.
I come through under pressure.

Bowling

I enjoy superior concentration. My arm is strong.
I follow through with my release. I pick up every spare.
I have the ability to string strikes together.

Football

I know where the ball is at all times. I run with high knees.
I am powerful. I have stamina. I visualize any motion.
I remain balanced and centered.

Martial Arts

My mind is clear. I breathe slowly and deeply.
I have flexible energy. I am aware and alert.
I visualize my motion. I remain balanced and centered.

Body-Building

I build my body to perfection. I exercise vigorously.
My workout gets results. My body is powerful.
I am strong. I am muscular. I am fit.

Golf

I play with confidence. I keep my head down.
My swing is powerful. I grip correctly.
I am a great golfer. I visualize success.

Soccer

I have tremendous speed.
I use my energy to control the game.
I am aware of the goalie's position.
I reach the ball before my opponent.

Tennis

I maintain smoothness and fluidity at all times.
I keep my body balanced on all strokes.
My footwork is excellent.
I am fast and move quickly to return the ball.

Running

My stride is long. My legs are strong.
My lungs expand. I breathe easily. My knees bend fluidly.
I am motivated to run. I love running.

Index

Abundance 38
Abuse, Surviving 7
Alcohol, Freedom from 56
Allergies, Freedom from 53
Anger, Dissolving 6
Appetite and Weight Control 42
Arthritis, Relief from 49
Assertive, Becoming 3
Athletic Performance, Winning 74
Attitude, Positive Mental 30
Awakening 21
Baseball 75
Basketball 75
Blood Pressure, Lower 50
Body Beautiful 58
Body-Building 77
Bowling 76
Brainpower, Hemispheric (Using Both Sides of the Brain) . .72
Burnout, Freedom from 35
Centering 23
Change, Accepting 6
Charisma 62
Charisma, Radiating Warmth and 9

Child Within, Rescripting the 4
Cholesterol, Reduce Naturally 43
Cigarettes, Forever Free of 50
Co-Dependent Patterns, Releasing 66
Commitment, Strong 31
Communication, Effective 8
Concentration, Powerful 68
Confidence 9
Confidence with the Opposite Sex 64
Connection 62
Consciousness Expansion 24
Creativity, Increase 17
Creativity, Unleash 16
Decide Now! Decide Right! 3
Depression, Free from 47
Dreamwork 17
Drug Prevention 57
Enlightenment 20
Enthusiasm and Motivation 2
Exams, Excel in 71
Exercise, Enjoying 54
Fears, Freedom from 5
Focus 70
Focus and Concentration 28

Football 76
Forgiveness 65
Forgiving and Letting Go 7
Goals, Setting and Achieving .26
Golf 78
Grades, Getting Good 69
Have It All 5
Headache Relief 51
Healing, Accelerating 56
Health, Imagine 47
Health, Radiant Good 46
Higher Power, Open Up to a .22
Higher Self 24
Humor, Great Sense of 10
Imagination and Visualization 18
Immune System, Powerful 48
Impulse Control 11
Intelligence, Super and Awakening Inner Genius 72
Intimacy, Enjoying and Sexual Self-Confidence 61
Intuition 18
Junk Food, Stop Eating 43
Learning 32
Learning, Peak 69

Longevity, Vitality and Health 44
Look Young! Feel Young! 44
Love, Attracting the Right Relationships 63
Love, Fulfillment in 61
Love, Light and Life 23
Management Skills 36
Martial Arts 77
Meditation 20
Memory Power 16
Memory, Powerful 68
Metaphysical Oneness 22
Miracles 21
Money Management, Successful 39
Motivated, Becoming 11
Motivation, Igniting Enthusiasm and 32
Neat and Clean 4
Networking for Successful Sales 35
Organized, Efficient and 26
Pain Relief, Natural 48
Pain Reduction 57
Parenting, Positive 63
Patience, Enduring 12
Performance, Peak 34

Personality, Winning 27
Posture, Excellent 54
Potential, High 40
Power, Unlimited Personal 31
Pregnancy and Childbirth, Joy of 45
Procrastinating, Stop 2
Prosperity 38
Prosperity and Success, Attracting 40
Reader, Becoming a Great 71
Recall 70
Recall, Powerful 29
Recharge 13
Recovery, Speeding after Injury or Operation 58
Relationships, Positive 65
Relaxation 52
Release 13
Running 79
Sales, Successful 34
Self-Confidence, Winning Self-Image 14
Self-Esteem, High 10
Self-Healing, Natural 51
Self-Image, Ultra-Positive 8
Self-Sabotage, Ending 66
Sexual Responsiveness for Men 60

Sexual Responsiveness for Women 60
Shyness, Overcoming 64
Skin, Clear 53
Sleep Soundly 52
Soccer 78
Speaking, Effective 29
Strategic Planning 36
Stress, Freedom from and Ultimate Relaxation 45
Study, Accelerated Learning and 69
Substance Abuse, Freedom from 49
Success, Enjoying 39
Success, Personal 27
Sugar, Freedom from 55
Tennis 79
Time, Managing Your 28
Trust 12
Vision, Keen 55
Vitality and Energy 46
Weight Loss, Winning at 42
Willpower 14
Winning State of Mind 30
Word Power 71
Yoga 74

Other products from Y.O.G.A. Productions

Journey Into New Dimensions

This one-hour meditation tape can help you achieve a quiet, relaxed, meditative state. Side One guides you in preparation for the meditation process, including breathing techniques. Side Two gives guided visualizations for morning and evening meditation. Louise-Diana narrates to soothing background music. $15.00

Seven Days to Your Own Greater Awareness: Y.O.G.A. for Everyone

This professionally produced 54-minute videotape presents a continuous set of yoga movements with complementary daily affirmations. Louise-Diana teaches the core principals of yoga simply, yet in a way that is true to tradition. Feel more alive and energized while gaining flexibility and reducing stress. Useful inspiration for the beginning student as well as the advanced adherent. $39.95

Affirmation Cards

A set of 50 affirmation cards that work together with this book. Small enough to carry to help keep you on track.

To order tapes make check payable to Y.O.G.A. Productions and mail to:
270 N. Canon Drive, Suite 1309, Beverly Hills, CA 90210 • 310-840-2253
(Include $2.50 for shipping. CA residents must add sales tax.)

www.innerfitness.com louise-diana@innerfitness.com